Published by
Enete Enterprises

1st edition of
Earn an Income Abroad

Enete, Shannon 2016

Earn an Income Abroad / Shannon Enete

ISBN-13: 978-1-938216-18-3
ISBN-10: 1-938216-18-0

Printed in the United States of America
www.EneteEnterprises.com

OTHER BOOKS BY THIS AUTHOR

Becoming an Expat **Costa Rica**
Becoming an Expat **Thailand**
Becoming an Expat **Mexico**
Becoming an Expat **Ecuador**
Becoming an Expat **101**
Becoming a **Nomad**
Becoming an Expat Costa Rica **Cookbook**
Teeth Not Tears: Smiles Through the Rubble

"This book was super helpful. Most books wade around the topic of earning an income abroad and only provide vague solutions, this one cuts through the bull and gets right down to it. It has tons of tips you can apply today to plan your financial escape. I highly recommend it."

~ Tara, California

"I've read a bunch of book on earning an income abroad or funding your travel, this one takes the cake. I particularly loved the worksheets that helped focus my passion and plan what type of freedom business I was best suited for. It really provided the guidance and practical tools I could actually use that the other books were lacking. Thanks!"

~ Brad, Florida

To those looking for their best lifestyle, to become the best version of themselves and do it all from their favorite place on earth.

DEDICATION

To all of my expat and nomadic friends and experts who have shared their experiences, helped answer questions, and demonstrated creative ways to co-exist on this planet.

A special thanks to my love, Gina Castagnozzi for her encouragement, kindness, and amazing support!

TABLE OF CONTENTS

Introduction

You aren't stuck. Every decision is a choice, including not making a decision and staying put. Your biggest hurdle is you. Feeling stuck is 100% mental. Life is fluid. Which is why we need to train ourselves to be flexible and work with change, not against it. You will soon learn how to discover your best business lifestyle and how to live in your favorite place on earth by either:

- The creation of a business anchored in your passions, life experience, and ideal lifestyle
- Travel-size your current job and take it on the road
- Go rogue and freestyle
- Realize a new career altogether that will allow you the necessary freedoms to earn a living while exploring the world.

Overall, I've been a very confident and determined individual. After a career-ending back injury, some of my confidence wavered. I functioned at the top of my peer group as a paramedic and without the consistent ego strokes, my confidence slowly waned. This caused a shift in my inner dialog and subconscious. Fear slid its ugly head into my life in a more powerful way than ever before. I found myself questioning every move I made: will it be profitable, will I fail? The fear of failure steered my decisions instead of passion and the pursuit of doing good. This experience isn't unique, most people who are stretching their limits and have stepped out of their comfort zone experience similar feelings and insecurities. Living out of our comfort zone is how we grow and leads to failure, then finally, success. Failure is usually a necessary stop on the road to success. After battling this shift, learning more about myself, and the journey of life, I stumbled upon some amazing tools that helped me rediscover my voice and the courage to execute what I believed in. I've shared them in this book because in order to Earn an Income Abroad, you will likely have to try on various businesses and opportunities before you find the right fit.

I can't tell you how often I hear, "Must be nice to travel all the time… I wish I could do that." or a variety of excuses stopping them, but they are just that— excuses. This is why I've dedicated the first chapter of this book to teaching you how to change your mentality, thought habits, redesign your attitude, and stifle your fear in order to have the confidence to get where you'd like to go. We even help you figure out where exactly that is!

Don't wait for retirement to actualize your dreams. There are no guarantees in life, and wouldn't you rather check off your bucket list experiences while you're health is good and you can hike, bike, walk, river raft, kayak, waterfall rappel, and any other crazy activity you'd like to tackle?

RETRAIN YOUR BRAIN

"Whether you think you can or you think you can't, you're right." ~ Henry Ford

What you believe about yourself is just that, a belief. It's not truth, but it's powerful non-the-less. If you were told you were a phenomenal singer growing up you could choose to agree and believe it or disagree and disregard the compliment saying something like, "they are just saying that to be nice" to yourself to reaffirm your belief that you are a poor singer. The power in this is we reaffirm what we believe about ourselves. To take my initial example, if I believe I'm a great singer then I will strive to be better and prove to myself and others that I'm awesome! If I believe I am a poor singer then I will shy away from practice and will never improve. You can see how this could impact our emotional, spiritual, and financial success. If we believe we are successful we will find a way to be successful.

"You are the average of the five people you spend the most time with." ~ Unknown

One of the best tips I've heard is to surround yourself with loving, supportive, and positive people. If you don't clean house of the people who bring you down with their negativity, it will be infinitely more difficult to replace your negative thoughts with positive ones. Think about it. How can you remain positive around a steady stream of negativity?

1. Think about your skill set. What beliefs do you have about your natural given gifts?

_____

_____

_____

_____

_____

2. What beliefs have you made about what is possible for you and your life?

_____

_____

_____

_____

_____

3. What new belief can you commit to make today? Where do you want your life to go? What skills would you like to develop? Take time and answer these questions thoroughly.

_____

_____

_____

_____

_____

_____

_____

_____

4. List the people in your life who are supportive of your goals and who have a positive attitude. People who align well with the person you are becoming.

_____

_____

_____

_____

_____

5. List the people who are negative and bring you down, or do not align with the best version of you.

_____

_____

_____

_____

_____

6. Look at the two sets of people and consider the amount of time you spend with each, see if you need to make any adjustments in order to live your Life Another Way. Remember, you are the average of the 5 people you spend the most time with.

_____

_____

_____

_____

_____

"Keep your thoughts positive because your thoughts become YOUR WORDS. Keep your words positive because your words become YOUR BEHAVIOR. Keep your behavior positive because your behavior becomes YOUR HABITS. Keep your habits positive because your habits become YOUR VALUES. Keep your values positive because your values become YOUR DESTINY." ~ Mahatma Gandhi

A poor attitude yields poor outcomes, a rich attitude leads to a rich life. Who is your negative attitude serving? You? Certainly not! Can you think of one good thing it's gotten you? Ask your loved ones how it impacts them when you are negative. If they're honest, you'll likely hear that when you're negative, you can be difficult to be around. It's like breathing in the smog-filled air, polluting their minds.

"Every thought we think is creating our future." ~ Louise Hay
"The mind is everything. What you think you become." ~ Buddha

A rich life is one where you thrive and are happy. While this often includes monetary riches, it doesn't have to if it's not part of your pursuit for happiness. Take the time you normally use to magnify what you're lacking and instead use it to focus on gratitude and what you're working towards. You will see massive transformation with this small shift in focus. Good begets good. Your positive attitude will not only bring you more happiness and freedom of mind but will provide opportunities and connections you'd never have as a negative Nancy.

Success is not 100% in your head, you have to have an attitude destined for success and put in the work. Whether you hail from the hard-working baby boomer generation or the more laissez faire millennial generation, you have to put in sweat equity to accomplish YOUR goals and YOUR best life. Think about it... What else would you want to put 100% effort into? This is not a math course you believe you'll never need again, this is a lesson that will teach you how to live your best life according to YOU! So don't half ass it!

TAKE RESPONSIBILITY

You want to live abroad right? You are the only one who is responsible for you and the only one who will take care of you. Don't hand over your happiness, life choices, or career to someone else. Don't let a boss, career, or other individual keep you from your goal if that goal is what you have decided is your top priority.

By placing your wellbeing and health into someone else's hands, you assign yourself a victim role. No matter what he/she/they choose to do for you, you're free to react with sadness and dismay. Avoid this at all cost! Placing someone else in charge of your happiness equals drama, pain, suffering, and a stuck or trapped facade. Why give away your power and outsource your happiness?

SHAPING YOUR NEW LIFE

In order to shape your life abroad with purpose you need to self-reflect and really get down to what it is you want out of life so you can muster the intention to arrive there.

How do you want to spend your days?

_____

_____

_____

_____

_____

What do you most like to do?

_____

_____

_____

_____

What kind of contribution do you want to make to the world?

_____

_____

_____

_____

_____

Where do you want to live if different from your current location?

_____

_____

_____

_____

_____

If you look at a question and can't decide between a few answers, write them all down. Now, with those answers in mind let's discover what the best day in your life would look like. Once we have a good grasp of your perfect day, we can work towards recreating it every single day with your ideal Earn an Income Abroad scenario! The more you document about your lifestyle goals, the stronger the blueprint we can build to get you there.

Here's an example:

"I wake up at 9am and walk to a lovely surf spot I live near. I enjoy surfing for an hour or so with my wife, then we walk back to our beachfront bungalow and enjoy a hot shower and cup of world class coffee. Then my wife and I discuss what we each want to get done that day. After we're done "accomplishing" (5-6 hours) we either go Stand Up Paddle boarding, kayaking, or on a leisurely hike. Then we enjoy dinner and a card game with a few of our closest friends."

With your answers in mind, describe your perfect day

_____

_____

_____

_____

_____

_____

_____

_____

_____

What do you need to change in your current life to open up the space for your ideal activities or that are in direct conflict with your new goals?

_____

_____

_____

_____

Looking at your perfect day, there are likely some aspects you can start right now. Who doesn't love immediate gratification? List the steps you can take right now.

_____

_____

_____

_____

Start introducing these "perfect moments" one by one into your life. For example, maybe your ideal life includes an after dinner walk, start this tradition now! The more things you can remove from your life that are inhibiting your goals, the more room you will have in your day for those moments you've deemed perfect for you. Inspect your life for activities that are "time sucks." Was watching TV part of your perfect day? If you spend your evenings watching TV, that's 5+ hours that could be spent doing something you love.

INCOME:

Think strategically here. Money is a means to an end, the end being your abroad. It's easy to get caught in a rouge money-hungry craze. How many people do you know hunt for money and success, then have no time or energy to spend it in the ways they envisioned in the first place. Keep your eye on the ball: the lifestyle, opportunities, and adventures the money you earn will afford you. Let money work for you, don't be a slave to money. Studies show that if you make $70,000 or more, money becomes less important and effects day to day stress and decision making less. If you have no idea how much money is enough for you, maybe this statistic could provide you a starting point.

How much money do you want to make monthly?

_____

How much money do you actually need each year?

_____

How much would your financial situation change if you worked from home?

_____

If you didn't need to work at all you would invest my time in:

These favorite activities:

_____
_____
_____
_____

These favorite places:

_____
_____
_____
_____

What 5 leisure activities would you like to see more of?

_____
_____
_____
_____

What 5 work-related activities would you like to see more of?

_____
_____
_____
_____

What 5 material objects would you like to see more of?

_____
_____
_____
_____

What 5 current job activities would you like to see less of?

_____
_____
_____
_____

What 5 current personal activities would you like to see less of?

_____
_____
_____
_____

What 5 people or types of people would you like to see less of?

_____
_____
_____
_____

In the next 6 months what are your top 5 things to change?

_____
_____
_____
_____

In the next 24 months what are the top 5 things you would like to see change?

_____
_____
_____
_____

YOUR FREEDOM BUSINESS

"Everything around you that you call life was made up by people that were no smarter than you and you can change it, you can influence it, you can build your own things that other people can use. Once you learn that, you'll never be the same again."

~ Steve Jobs

Have you ever considered starting a business and being your own boss? In your years on this earth you have developed a compilation of skills, hobbies, and experiences that are unique to you. You have something others need. Listen to what people compliment you on, it's often something they notice because they lack it and they admire it in you. You can either work really hard to realize someone else's dream or you can reap the benefits of *your* sweat equity.

You're the architect of your life and by starting a freedom business you'll have full control of its successes and failures. In this book, you'll learn what type of business is the right fit for you and the steps required in order to transform a good idea into a thriving business.

As you brainstorm, make a concerted effort to have an open mind. There are thousands of ways to earn an income. We will demonstrate a variety of business models, so take notes if one resonates with you. Dream big! Remember this life is based on your loves and passions, not what you're supposed to do. Also, don't focus on the money. It's an easy trap. Focus on a need or problem that you can fill/fix. Passion + Problem resolution = \$\$\$

COMMON MYTHS

The stigma of being a business owner can be frightening, but that's all it is, a stigma.

I'M NOT AN EXPERT

We will teach you how to become and leverage yourself as an expert in your field in under 30 days. People don't want to be taught by the best in a field, they want someone they can relate with. Someone that will speak to them in a clear concise manner. Someone who will give them the shortcuts they wish they'd known about when they were just starting out. If you were recently in their place, you can relate in a way that most experts can't.

I DON'T HAVE AN MBA

A Masters in Business Administration teaches you how to work for someone else and make *them* money.

Leveraging your skills, expertise, experience, and ability to learn and adjust will make you a successful business owner and entrepreneur. We'll show you just how to do it.

I DON'T HAVE ENOUGH $$

Starting a business doesn't take cash, it takes guts and the willingness to leave your comfort zone. If your business idea requires initial capital to get started, there are plenty of ways to access those funds. You could start a Kickstarter campaign, reach out to family and friends, or take advantage of the cheap cost of living abroad to give your budget the breathing room it needs in order to launch your business.

Plan ahead, utilize free money saving tools like those offered at your bank where you can set up an automatic weekly or monthly transfer of money into your business nest egg account.

When I wanted to visit New Zealand in my 20s, I got a side job where I worked about 10-12 hours a week. I put all of my earnings from this second job into a New Zealand fund. You could do the same for a business account (covering expenses such as business research, training, marketing, and development).

Ideas, determination, expertise, and execution are much more critical to the success of a business. There are countless examples of companies who started up in a garage for less than a hundred bucks, Apple Computers being one of them.

FREEDOM

When considering life's freedoms, it's hard to top being your own boss. The social and technological inventions over the past decade have brought us near the "End of Jobs" while making entrepreneurship safer, more accessible, and more profitable than ever before. With a shrinking middle class and no guarantees from our employers, why not take matters into your own hands?

"In 2020, there will be 40% more 25–34 year olds with higher education degrees from Argentina, Brazil, China, India, Indonesia, Russia, Saudi Arabia, and South Africa than in all OECD countries (a group of 34 countries primarily in Western Europe and North America)."

~ Taylor Pearson, The End of Jobs: Money, Meaning and Freedom Without the 9-to-5

Your high school and much of your college education isn't designed to teach you how to start your own venture, instead your education was geared towards teaching you how to make others rich. This book will teach you practical skills you can apply NOW. Your first business could fail, or you could be wildly successful. **Failure is just a brief pit stop en route to success, keep driving!**

Since 2000, the population has grown 2.4 × faster than jobs opportunities. You can see why the last few graduating classes have had such a hard time finding jobs. Maybe it's time to create your own job.

Why even consider taking on such a big project and such grave responsibility?

Pros and cons lists always help me sort my thoughts. Below you'll find a pros and cons list that is geared towards the decision to start your own freedom business or not:

PROS

- Work from home, whether that's in Bali, Tuscany, or Chicago
- No commute! Unless you want one, in which case, have at it
- Take vacations, sick days, personal days…whatever you need whenever you need it. You are in charge of your own time and your days are yours
- Help out with the family and nurture your marriage (if applicable)
- Enjoy a hike, swim, surf, kayak, or walk during your lunch break (mid-week while the masses are stuck at work)
- Move to a better climate
- Do what you're passionate about and what you hold important
- Change and adapt as your passions and interests change. You can be flexible and continue to evolve your work as it

suits you, without having to change jobs or get approval from a boss

- Rid of busy-work forever
- Make money doing things you'd usually pay to do. (i.e. If you love playing pool and you start a business as an online pool and billiards retailer, it's now part of your job to hang out with your heroes (the top pool players in the world) or fly around the world to speak on your consulting topics such as entrepreneurship or strategy)

CONS

- No steady or guaranteed paycheck— This one is a biggie and often the biggest hurdle from your dream freedom business
- You are solely responsible for your successes and failures (there is no one else to blame or hide behind)
- Usually more demanding (especially during it's conception, launch, and infancy)
- You will be kicked out of your comfort zone and challenged from many fronts (this is also a pro)

LIFESTYLE

THE ENTREPRENEUR'S WORK WEEK

"I had thought that by focusing on business and money I was making myself free, but I didn't understand that freedom requires more balance than that. At that point, I knew that if I was going to truly be free, if I was really going to be liberated from work, I needed to

focus on ways to reduce the amount of time I spent maintaining my business, and to increase the amount of time I had to focus on what I should really be doing with my life. I knew then that freedom is not just going towards." ~ Erlend Bakke, Never Work Again: Work Less, Earn More and Live Your Freedom

I have a secret for you... Working less hours doesn't mean you're less productive. In fact for me, working 5-6 hours per day 4-5 days a week is my sweet spot! I'm the most productive because I'm energized and excited about my work. I avoid burnout and have plenty of time in my day to hike, surf, and enjoy loved ones. I find that when I push myself to work after my mind and body are done, it's counterproductive in a variety of ways. However, there are days I'm on fire and I'll ride that wave into a 12 hour day. More often than not, the aftershock of such a day is a few days off to bask in the glory of my productivity. That's the balance that I've found, what does yours look like? If your not sure, don't worry we'll work on that later.

WHAT ABOUT 9-5 AND TIME ZONES?

Who says you're glued to a 9am-5pm workday? Maybe a new time zone is exactly what you need to take advantage of mornings to explore a new city or to enjoy afternoons off to catch a wave. Perhaps your ideal schedule will be 5am-1pm. Sure, that's an early start! But if you finish working at 1pm, think of all that daylight time you have for adventures!

Or maybe you will work 2pm-10pm, which would allow you to sleep in and enjoy a leisurely breakfast before heading out to see what the world has to offer. Key take home message, A 9-5 work schedule is not the only option! Most industries don't require a response within the same 12 hours, so if you're a few hours off, it's usually not critical to your business. If you're working remotely for a corporation that you don't own then you may have a required set schedule, however, you can decide what time zone to work from and how to manipulate it to your best advantage.

GETTING STARTED

If you know for certain you have zero interest in starting your own business you can either skip ahead or skim through for the golden nuggets you can apply to any life.

GLOBALIZING YOUR INCOME

"Today, on average, people will change their career 8 times before they turn 40... Employers are no longer loyal to employees for their lifetime, nor are employees loyal to employers in the same way." ~ Nora Dunn, The Professional Hobo, a finance and self-sustaining travel guru podcast interview

Regardless of whether your business sells a product or supplies a service, you can run it seamlessly from anywhere in the world. Plenty of people are taking their businesses overseas: digital marketers, graphic designers, eCommerce entrepreneurs, online publishers, writers, teachers, etc. Maybe it's a different climate you seek, a different pace of life, a new and unique culture, or a more affordable cost of living. Maybe you just want to enjoy a new place for a few months out of the year.

Not only can you save thousands in overhead and improve your quality of life by starting a business abroad, you're also free to explore any destination in the world. Let that realization soak in...

I've lived in Costa Rica, Ecuador, Peru, Thailand, and travel through countless countries around the world, all from which I was able to manage and run my business. I can't tell you how refreshing it is to know I can pack up my belongs in just a few minutes and relocate to work in a new exotic country as often as I'd like. For many, bliss comes with the combination of a home-base and a healthy dose of exploration abroad. There is NO reason why you can't have this too!

Dream Big, Act Small

Sounds a bit unproductive, but stick with me. Your goals should encompass the big picture, the life you designed and all its glory. Your actions or steps toward this goal should be the minimum amount of work you need to accomplish each given day. This way the goal becomes achievable.

Routines & Habits United

When trying to introduce a new habit, work with your routine instead of against it. That way you can create environmental triggers to remind you to act on your new habit. For instance, if you want to snack less and exercise more, you could decide to do 10 pushups every time you open the refrigerator door. You might even save money on your electric bill! The secret sauce here is the fact you rely on contextual cues instead of willpower.

Eliminate Excessive Options

You make thousands of choices everyday. How much energy do you really want to spend deciding what you wear and what to eat for each meal or snack? President Obama limits his suits to just blue or grey. This way he doesn't have to make decisions about what he's wearing because he says, "...I have too many other decisions to make." If you want to maintain long term discipline, it's best to routinize mundane aspects of your life so you can spend less energy making decisions.

Visualize the End Game & the Route to It

While visualization is powerful, if you also visualize the process required to obtain your goal, its power multiplies. For example, if your end-game is a muscular and toned body with 10% body fat, instead of solely visualizing your body in pristine condition, also visualize working out in the gym each day, sweating and enjoying the labor of love for your body. This not only reduces any anxiety you may have about achieving your goals, it helps focus your attention on the steps required to reach them.

Eliminate "Ah-screw-its"

It's January 5th, you made a New Year resolution to go to the gym 3x a week, and yet you're in bed when you should be half way through your workout. Why? Did you feel the warm comfort of your bed and say, "Ah-screw-it"? Then, when your adherence streak was over, did you just give up? Why are we so quick to abandon new habits?

There are specific road blocks between us and our goals. The more accurate we are in determining where the roadblocks are, the better our chances at adherence to our new habits and goal achievement.

YOUR FUTURE BUSINESS

Deciding what type of business to start can be a daunting and intimidating task, so let's break it down to the bare bones. Never focus on what you don't have, instead focus on what you do have because it's all you need to accomplish these three critical components:

1. A product or service that solves a problem. *"It's easier and cheaper than ever to make something and tell people about it."* ~ Pearson, The End of Jobs
2. A group of people who will pay for it
3. A way to take their money

FINDING YOUR SWEET SPOT

Make a list of what you love doing. List as many things as possible. What would you do if money was not a factor?

For example: Dance, sew, pour coffees, give advice, listen, solve problems, paint, write, speak for events, connect people (networking), solve IT problems, throw parties, fundraise, etc.

LISTEN TO OTHERS

What do people tell you you're naturally good at? Instead of being modest and dismissing compliments from your network, tune in. Pay special attention to what they're saying. They've recognized something in you that you take for granted but they find useful and valuable enough to tell you about it. When your friends or colleagues say *"You're really good at _____"* take note. Create a list of the things people say you're good at:

A. Organizing parties
B. Playing matchmaker
C. Cooking
D. Simplifying the complex
E. Running fundraisers
F. Interior design
G. Making people laugh

Now take a look at the two lists you've created (what you love to do and what others tell you you're good at) and explore which areas people have a need and already pay good money to access.

For example, if you love to cook and have been told by many that your food is amazing and tastes fresh or top notch, you might consider a catering business. You can find a model that satiates your work:play ratio (discussed in detail in our core-pack course), such as home delivery 2 days a week or special events (but only allow 1 event per week and price accordingly).

Finding Your Sweet Spot Worksheet:

Answer each one of the following questions twice, once for each of your top two business ideas.

1. Describe your business idea in two-three sentences

_____
_____
_____
_____
_____
_____
_____
_____
_____
_____

2. Describe how your business would generate income

_____
_____
_____
_____
_____
_____
_____
_____
_____
_____
_____
_____

3. What business foundation would your business primarily rely on? (which P)

_____
_____
_____
_____
_____
_____
_____

_____
_____

4. How is your business different than its competition?

_____
_____
_____
_____
_____
_____
_____
_____
_____
_____
_____

5. How does your business idea scale? What does growth look like, and how is it accomplished?

_____
_____
_____
_____
_____
_____
_____
_____
_____
_____

6. What will it take to start your business?

_____
_____
_____
_____
_____
_____
_____
_____
_____
_____

BUILDING YOUR FOUNDATION

There are many directions you can take when building the scaffolding of your freedom business. You start by deciding which one of the the four P's fuel your company concept: Passion, People, Problem, or a Product.

Passion: Is your business based on a passion? (i.e. hobby, issues, industry, or a cause you feel is important to promote.)

People: Think about what type of person you enjoy spending time with.

Problem: Observe problems, inconveniences, or needs in your own daily life.

Product: Do you know about a product that deserves a wider audience? Or do you have a new product, service, or information that you'd like to market?

Make a note here identifying which business foundation (or P) resonates with you. Then write down 5+ business ideas and identify which foundation (P) each would use. We're just brainstorming so don't be critical, just spit balling here so write the ideas that come to you.

YOUR FOUNDATION & CORRESPONDING IDEAS

STRESS-TEST YOUR BUSINESS IDEA

Whose needs are you fulfilling?

Let's carry your foundation a step further and consider whose needs you would be fulfilling? How do you reach them (blogs, forums, noozles, podcast, videos, webinars, apps, etc)?

What are their top needs you could make money satisfying? Once you have a grasp on what their needs are you need to determine their preferred method to receive information. For example, if your target audience is retirees then noozles, podcasts, and blogs might not reach a lower tech generation.

Does your target audience have purchasing power?

Does your target audience spend money on what you plan to offer? What's their purchasing power? If your target audience doesn't have purchasing power is there a government grant you could qualify for? For example: pet owners have a range of purchasing power. If your target audience is gay pet owners or power professional pet owners then their spending power is practically limitless. They treat their pets like family members and have no problem opening up their wallet if the product will serve a need for their pet. If your target audience is pet shelters then you may need to find a way to fundraise or apply for grants in order to get your product/service in their hands.

Narrow down your business ideas to the Top 2. Test each idea with the following exercises. If none seem feasible, head back to step one and start over. Time is much better spent starting over now than after pouring countless hours and resources into a business that won't produce. The average business owner has 2-3+ failed business attempts before he/she reaches the one that works for them and their customers.

Once you've whittled down your list, research your competition and similar products or services in other markets. Can you improve on what they're doing? Treat this research like a cafeteria plan. Take away the best practices of each business model you research.

What key practices did you observe that you want to implement in your business model?

_____
_____
_____
_____
_____
_____
_____
_____
_____
_____

What can you do to differentiate yourself so that people will want to read your blog, watch your videos, buy your products or services, etc?

_____
_____
_____
_____
_____
_____

Which items, services, or concepts provide you with the best opportunity to make money and align with your top

priorities for daily living? Asked another way... If 1,000 fans paid you $100 a piece annually, what would you do for them?

_____
_____
_____
_____
_____
_____
_____
_____
_____
_____
_____
_____
_____
_____
_____
_____

HOW TO BECOME AN EXPERT

To be considered an expert in any given skill you don't have to be the best at it, you just have to be better than others who want to learn. When you're one step further along you can not only be marketed as an expert but can really help those that are walking behind you. People don't want to be taught by the best in a field, they want someone who can relate and has put in the sweat equity. Someone who will speak to them in their language, who remembers what they are going through. Someone who share shortcuts they wish they would have had when they were at point A. If you recently learned a marketable skill, you can relate in a way that most experienced experts cannot.

Let's be practical, knowing is half the battle. You also have to market your knowledge and create a platform. This usually requires the creation of a website that features your services and experience while simultaneously creating a professional "storefront." Blogging or video blogging is one easy way to establish yourself as an expert. By providing valuable or helpful content to your target audience you become a resource for them. Even if you didn't write all of the articles, instead you set a couple of google alerts with topics that you are an expert in and peruse the articles that come to your inbox for the best quality and most helpful in your industry. Then simply share them to your site in a blog or resource tab and you become a place where people can head for the best resources on the given topic so they don't have to sort through all of the minutia themselves.

$$ FUNDING A STARTUP

There are a variety of ways to fund a new business. If you have a large nest egg or family money then you're likely not reading this book. So let's move on. Some opt to keep their day job, so-to-speak until their startup is producing in a way that is more reliable as a singular income. This can be challenging and we'll address the pros and cons below in a bit. In today's age crowdfunding is a huge new way to test and fund new ventures. Instead of sitting in meetings with suits and venture capitalists who will essentially own your soul you can throw your idea to the masses through a well crafted video and prototype and see if there is demand while simultaneously funding production!

When you consider which method would be the best fit to fund your startup remember one key fact. Living abroad means you can drastically decrease your overhead so your required income during your startup phase could be drastically lower if you opt to start up from the Philippines, Thailand, Ecuador, Peru, or other affordable country. You can also be creative with your budget by including housesitting gigs (decreasing or getting rid of your rental expenses), trade your new business product/service (to gain more referrals and to build your working portfolio), and other part time work to score free food or other beneficial partnership.

Part Time Start Up- *don't quit your day job*

In order to start a business you simply need a service or product and someone willing to pay for it. You can start a business part-time with a few people you've found that need your offering. You can fill that need before your business structure and website are even developed. In fact, learning from those who need your services with a few guinea pig runs then asking for feedback before you set your structure in place is EXTREMELY beneficial.

Bootstrapping

Instead of saving loads of money or finding a venture capitalists to fund your business, bootstrapping your startup is a shoestring way to start a business. Basically, you pay for everything you need as you need it. No investment egg, instead you grow very slowly and only according to your financial ability, without the use of huge loans or partners. Keeping your overhead low and logistics as simple as possible is the only way this will work. Typically we're talking a 1-2 person operation here.

Crowdfunding

Different crowdfunding sites like "Kickstarter" have become a great way to launch/test a product or service. With little work you can create just enough for a prototype and professional video of your offering, then create a fundraising goals and share with the masses. If you reach your goal you are successful and definitely onto something big.

REVENUE STREAMS

How do you make money on each product/service is a revenue stream. For example, if you write a book and sell it on Amazon you can create passive income through the royalties of that book. If the book introduces a coaching program, or other service you offer then you have an additional revenue stream from the book that leads to sales of your service or product. Below are a few more examples of potential revenue streams:

- Services- Like coaching, consulting, copywriting, web design
- Products— Either digital products and programs, books, software, apps, merchandise, instructional videos, and consumer goods
- Affiliates— Promoting others people/company's products, programs or services
- Sponsorship— For events, products, your blog/ podcast/ YouTube videos
- Speaking Engagement
- Events— Workshops, retreats, conferences
- Subscriptions— member only newsletters, blog, Facebook community, access to other resources

The examples above include both passive and active revenue streams. Passive streams pay you multiple times for work you did once (i.e. Book sales, product sales). While there's still marketing work required to maintain sales, these revenue streams are much less labor intensive than their counterpart. For example: to run an event or service one sale equals one payment (active revenue), whereas selling digital products you create the product once and sell it many times over.

Ideally, you want to find a way to have a few different revenue streams and repackage your offerings in various ways in order to reach the largest audience and produce the best return.

FINANCIAL GOALS

How much money do you want?

Sounds like a silly question, but it's important to be intentional with your financial goals. Earlier we asked what you would do if money didn't matter, now we've come full circle to ask you how much money do you actually want? A lot is not the answer. Decide what the minimum amount you need to earn in order for you to be satisfied. What income would free your mind from being a slave to money. The dollar amount that lends you to the simple and satisfying life you desire. If you are unsure about the amount, take a couple of hours to create a budget that includes what you'd like and what you need to be satisfied.

Studies have shown $70,000 to be the US national average where people no longer feel restricted by their income.

_____
_____
_____
_____
_____
_____
_____

WHAT WILL IT TAKE TO LAUNCH

How much time and money do you estimate it will take before you're profitable?

_____
_____
_____
_____
_____
_____
_____

What recurring operating costs do you anticipate?

_____
_____
_____

How much of the business requires regular updating (i.e. website, content, marketing, etc)?

_____
_____
_____
_____
_____
_____
_____

What can be automated by software?

_____
_____
_____
_____
_____

_____

_____

Can you hire someone else to replace you down the road or does it require your personal attention?

_____

_____

_____

Is there a way to have your audience contribute content?

_____

_____

_____

How can you scale this business? Will it scale automatically or will you need to pour more resources into it?

_____

_____

_____

_____

_____

_____

_____

BUSINESS RESOURCES

COMMUNICATION

Business would not exist without communication. Your business may require both local and international communication options. Let's begin with telephone communication. There are a variety of internet-based phone solutions that are both economic and affective. Your internet connection will be hit or miss on the road. Skype and magicJack are excellent options for an international phone solution. Utilizing email and social media to keep up with your clients is another nice way to circumvent a crummy connection.

You can purchase a phone number with the desired country and area code for an annual fee (my fee this year was $60) through Skype. You could then forward your calls to funnel through one phone with the use of Google Voice. If you plan to serve the local community you will need to a local number, most likely a cell phone for smaller operations. This way you can funnel different numbers for varies services you may offer.

When I purchased a US number from Skype, I was also provided with three-way calling, group video conferencing, and a personal voicemail. As with any internet phone service, there are glitches from time to time. I've had a few instances where my voicemail didn't pick up and my client was unable to leave a message, but it is a rare occurrence.

Before Skype international calls were incredibly expensive. Calling cards and international plans were the most cost effective solutions. With Skype, you can buy a subscription for just about any type of unlimited calling you desire: North America, Latin America, and world wide all starting at $2.99 per month!

If you have a smartphone with a local sim card installed, download the Skype app. Once you're logged in and have a strong connection to the internet through either cellular or wifi, you are able to use all of your Skype features on the go!

Living or traveling to the Caribbean, Ecuador, or Thailand doesn't mean you're faced with insurmountable hurdles communicating with your team or clients. In fact, with a Skype number and an unlimited international calling subscription, it's just as if you were in your home country.

VIRTUAL OFFICE

You'll need to set up a virtual office system that works. Whether you are working from cafes with wifi or the family home, decide what time of day you're most productive and work your schedule around that time.

OVERHEAD

Less is more. Your goal is to be rid of all leases, landlines, and file-cabinets. Get used to the idea that your "office" can consist of you lounging in a hammock with a cellphone, laptop, and wifi connection. I've even worked from a beach chair in the sand— risky, and the screen was hard to read with the bright sun, but so worth it! Working from my hammock (covered with a tiki roof) overlooking the pool and the perfectly manicured jungle surrounding it, worked out much better than the beach.

Your virtual office could be inside of an internet cafe in any country around the world, on a train, plane, or in a home office in your new tropical abode. Whatever environment you choose, you'll need a reliable internet connection (via wifi or hotspot), smartphone, laptop, and a few applications that will help your workflow. My favorite "office" is a local coffee shop (as long as they have a cozy seating setup).

PROGRAMS THAT CONNECT

Google Hangouts, GoToMeeting, and Skype are all excellent platforms for video conferencing.

Slack is a new program that coordinates communication amongst teams. It's like AOL's Instant Messenger on steroids. With hashtags (#) you can organize and search conversations. So if you need to talk to your graphic designer about a project you can either #project name or #design to organize your conversation. It integrates with Asana (mentioned below) and a variety of other programs. The best part is it's free!

SHARING

Never has it been so easy to share files with colleagues and clients or even across your own devices.

Dropbox keeps your team's documents backed-up and accessible. By saving them on dropbox.com you can share folders, docs, and access them from any computer or smart device around the world. No more headaches when your computer crashes! Plus, now you can sell your bulky file-cabinets. Google Gmail, Google Calendar, Google Keep, Google Drive, Google Docs, Gmail Offline, Google Hangouts and numerous other Google apps that integrate with Google and gmail will simplify your life and sync across all of your devices.

Asana is an excellent online tool used to organize projects, to-dos, and keep clear conversations with your staff without the use of email. I used this platform to organize the creation of Life Another Way as well as manage its daily needs.

You won't likely have access to a Kinkos if you're traveling or living abroad. Granted, most of us no longer use fax machines, so you may run into potential challenges when it comes to signing documents. Luckily, there are numerous programs that allow you to fax your documents (such as hello fax) from your computer or smart phone and apply a digital signature to documents (Preview on a Mac, Hello Sign on any device). These programs make signing contracts, leases, and other documents a breeze from anywhere in this world. Here is an article that walks you through electronic signatures for those who have never entered this world.

Believe it or not, you can even have a document notarized online! Use notarycam.com and speak with a notary via webcam, verify your identity with a few background questions and bam, you've got a notarized document without leaving your couch or favorite coffee shop. I didn't believe it until I tried it. To my surprise it worked beautifully!

BOOKKEEPING

Being creative and productive is one thing, but it's vitally important to keep track of your invoicing and accounts. You want to see the money coming in.

Freshbooks (starting at $9.95) is an easy, non-intimidating way to tackle your accounting with tools that will track your time, create invoices, manage your expenses and more. Plus, your books are always backed up on their cloud.

Shoeboxed ($10-100 p/mo) is a painless scanning system. Pile your receipts and docs into one of their blue envelopes and send away! Also you can integrate your gmail, outlook, and other email providers so that your receipts are automatically sent to Shoebox, filed, and stored away. They will sort, scan, and organize all of your documents and business cards into an electronic system that will save you time, organize your life, and lift the weight (from piles of paper) off your shoulders and desk. Moreover, their human data verification makes your documents searchable. They can even create expense reports and track mileage for you through an app on your smartphone.

SUPPORT, OUTSOURCING, & EMPLOYEES

Regardless if you're a solepreneur or you employ an army, creating a virtual team is a no-brainer. Gone are the days when you have to supply a computer, printer, fax machine, and landline to each of your employees. You just saved thousands in overhead with one decision.

There are a variety of administrative support options available virtually. Packages range from answering services to full-time virtual assistants (VAs). Answering services start at just $0.80 a day including a friendly operator answering the phone with your company's name. Afterwards, they either forward the call or take a message then email and/or fax the message to you. ReceptionHQ has an iPhone app that allows you to change receptionist settings and diversion numbers from anywhere in the world. They offer a free seven day trial. Try out a few companies before you leave the country.

By giving your employees location independence and freedom studies show employees they will be significantly more productive and happy with their job. You can either keep them on as full-time location independent employees or reorganize your staffing needs with virtual assistants (VAs), independent contractors, or outsource your administrative and specialized needs. Hiring full-time employees is much more expensive and complicated from an HR standpoint. Take care in your decisions regarding labor and growth of your company.

VIRTUAL ASSISTANTS

A virtual assistant (VA) is exactly what it sounds like, a private secretary that works from his/her home. They can answer and respond to phone calls, filter through and answer your emails, and redirect the ones that require your special attention. Common tasks also include: booking your travel, managing your personal and professional calendar, managing social media, blogging, chat room presence, and running down leads.

Tim Ferriss emphasized the usefulness of VAs in his book The 4-Hour Work Week. One example of a VA company is EAHelp. They provide an executive assistant starting with as little as five hours a week.

Upwork.com (previously Elance & Odesk), peopleperhour.com, freelancer.com, and fiverr.com are excellent websites to find independent contractors or to hire a virtual team. You can pay them per hour or automatically charge your credit card after you've seen and approved their work. That way you spend time doing what you do best, and save the stress and headache of the things you aren't proficient in by hiring those who are. I have had great luck hiring people from Upwork and Fiverr that were based out of India and Pakistan. It's been cost effective and incredibly simple.

SOPs

By creating standard operating procedures (SOPs) for those things you'd like to outsource, you can equip others with the instructions to do the work exactly as you'd like them to be completed from anywhere in the world. Outsourcing has been a game changer for the world, and certainly for me.

INTERNATIONAL BANKING

If you want to travel for a living or live abroad, you need to pay special attention to your bank's fees. Re-evaluate your current bank with the following criteria designed to suit your new life:

- Can you fax a wire request to transfer money?
- Are there ATM fees, if so are they excessive?
- What is the currency transaction fee?
- If you are receiving a pension, Social Security, or annuity, can the payments be automatically deposited to your current bank? www.ssa.gov/foreign/index.html
- Do they offer mobile deposits?
- Are they FDIC insured?
- Is there a minimum balance requirement to avoid maintenance fees?
- Fees

Most banks charge a foreign transaction fee (a percentage of your purchase) each time you swipe your debit or credit card for a bill that is in a currency other than that of your country of origin. For example, if your bank charges a 10% currency transaction fee (CTF) and you buy dinner for $35 USD, your currency transaction fee will be $3.50 USD! CTFs add up quickly as do ATM fees.

I didn't think to change banks before I moved to CR. In just 6 months of living in Costa Rica, I racked up $210.67 USD in fees just to access my money! I now proudly bank with Charles Schwab and pay zero fees (information to follow).

Check to see what your bank charges each time you access your money from an "out of network" ATM. More often than not, the bank whose ATM you are using will also apply a fee. You could be looking at anywhere between $5-10 USD just to use the ATM! If you are withdrawing currency other than the US Dollars, tack on the Foreign Transaction Fee.

You'll likely conclude your bank will not serve you well as an international resource. I have banked with Bank of America, Washington Mutual, and most recently Wells Fargo. I was paying way to much to access my money internationally, so I did some research and found a bank that offers everything I was looking for. Charles Schwab's High Yield Investor's Checking Account. (I do not receive any kickbacks from CS.)

Take a look at the benefits:

- Zero maintenance fees
- Zero minimum balance requirement
- ZERO CURRENCY TRANSACTION FEES
- Free brokerage account
- Mobile deposits
- Online banking
- UNLIMITED ATM FEE REIMBURSEMENTS- not only do they not charge ATM fees of their own, they take it one step further and reimburse you for the fees other banks charge to use their ATMs to access your money around the world!
- FDIC insured up to $250,000!

Getting paid is critical! It's incredibly easy to get paid online. Especially if you can use a US bank account. Some methods require a card reader, others integrate with your website. You can send out invoices, and even get paid by email! Below, I've highlighted my favorite small business friendly ways to receive payments.

Paypal— Using Paypal, you can add a buy now or subscription button to your website, you can bill via invoice, and send and receive money via a simple email. In order to utilize all of their options you need to have it linked with a US bank. You can even get a debit/credit card to pull out money from your Paypal account, or transfer money into your preferred bank account. You will pay at least
Fees: 2.7%.

Gmail— If your bank is located in the US or UK you can use the fairly new Google Wallet to send and receive money via gmail! Simply compose your email, attach $ (instead of or in addition to a document), then if you're sending money enter the amount you want to send and choose a funding source or if you're requesting money click Request at the top of the box and enter the amount you're requesting. Then if everything looks right hit send!

Flint— Flint offers a simple, professional, and handy way to receive funds with very competitive rates. One of my favorite features is that no card reader is necessary! You can charge cards by hand, receiving online payments, and send invoices. They have a great user friendly app to take on the road. There is no merchant or start up fees, no monthly fees, and no penalizing for hand entered charges. A straight forward 1.95% fee for debit cards and 2.95% for credit cards. Plus, the money will drop into your account within 1-2 business days! Personally, I like the flexibility this route offers, and the control over pricing and coupon codes. They do not yet offer a way to automate subscriptions, I hope they add this feature in the near future.

Square—An early leader in small business banking. The square card reader is simple to use plugging into the headset port on any smart phone. They also have a popular stand that transforms any iPad into a high tech cash register. They charge a 2.75%-3.5% fee per transaction. There are no setup fees and they offer a $250 monthly chargeback protection for payment disputes.

Additional Resources:

Books: Suitcase Entrepreneur, Start a Freedom Business, The End of Jobs: Money, Meaning, and Freedom Without the 9-to-5, 4-Hr Work Week
Blogs: Jet Citizen, The Perfect Workspace According to Science
Podcasts: Business Basecamp, Suitcase Entrepreneur, Achieve Your Goals

GROW YOUR BUSINESS

Absolutely everything you do to grow your business must:

- Add value to your customers
- Connect (or make sense) to your target audience

MARKETING STRATEGY
Understanding Your Target Audience

I don't watch a lot of television but when I do, I enjoy watching shows like The Profit or Shark Tank because it's an entertaining way to learn what works and what doesn't and draw from the experience of some successful businessmen/ women. An error I've seen made time and time again by young business owners is not understanding or correctly identifying and marketing to their target audience. This is critical. How can you pitch your product or service effectively without understanding the needs and location of your market? More over if you understand their needs but have no idea how to reach them then how will you convert sales, add value, and solve problems?

NETWORKING

Network. You don't have to be in the same room with people to get to know them. Use social media and email to reach out and build your community of influence. Networking is more about being helpful than asking people to help you.

Guest blogging is a great way to network. If you have a great article you'd like to share with other outlets that serve a common interest, share away! You will provide them with high quality free content catered to their market all while building your audience and extending your reach. Make sure and have a link back to your website in your byline.

GROW YOUR BUSINESS MODEL

Remember earlier in the course when we discussed various revenue streams? When you're looking to grow your business one key way to increase revenue is to find a way to repackage what you're already doing into services / products that fall into more revenue streams.

For example, if you own a consultation company you could package a course, book, and create a membership community to take advantage of passive income through book and course sales, and level up into the reoccurring fee world with your paid community!

The lower your overhead the higher your freedom.

Growing your business does not mean growing your overhead substantially. Keep your overhead as low as permitted. Avoid the pressures to scale up your expenses. Even if your business takes off. Make smart purchases, like adding an independent contractor, virtual assistant, and delegating tasks away from your desk to those individuals so that you can focus on what you do best, bringing in more business. Just because you can afford a fancy office doesn't mean you should lease one.

AUTOMATION

A critical component when scaling a company is automation. Each task required to run your business should be evaluated in order to determine if it could and should be automated. The more automated your tasks are the more free your life is, and the more scalable your business becomes.

I'm not talking about becoming robots or less personal, I'm simply recommending you to utilize software and technology where it makes sense. For instance, if you have a membership group, allow Paypal or other software to do the heavy lifting (automatically charging your members monthly and providing them their login credentials without any interaction or work on your part). Sure there will be hiccups here and there but that is what customer service is for! Many software programs and services (like Paypal) offer this direct customer service for you and YOUR customers. This is one of many examples where you can work smarter not harder.

RECURRING REVENUE

I LOVE passive income, but the real heavy hitter is recurring revenue. It's super difficult to build any business without recurring revenue or repeat business. So if you can find any way to offer regular value for a membership community you're golden.

For this to work you need to have a community of fans. If you're new to the game, offer membership free for the first 50 people. You will rely on them to spread the word about how useful, educational, inspiring, or otherwise your community is. Once again success will come down to are you providing true value and are you connecting with those who can benefit from it the most?

BE FLEXIBLE

Be patient and flexible. Everything takes longer than you think. Have realistic expectations and don't expect to be an overnight sensation. Measure the effectiveness of your actions. That way you know if you need to make adjustments.

If your plan is not producing or meeting your realistic goals try a new tactic or revamp your plan all together. Ask your customers/clients what is working, where they find value and how you can improve, what else they would like to see from you. Focus your growth on this, if at first you miss the mark, don't force it, listen clearly to your clients and revamp your plan.

PART II
REMOTE WORK
TRAVE-SIZE YOUR CAREER

REMOTE WORK

"When I'm sitting in front of my computer it doesn't really look like work, but it is because it pays the bills."
~Nora Dunn, The Professional Hobo

Working remotely comes with many names: telework, telecommute, work from home, location independent...and the list goes on. They all mean is the same thing: more freedom. Telecommuting has increased by 80% from 2005 to 2012.

Freeing up your office location means you can literally work from anywhere in the world. Technology has improved to the point that you can literally work from the the other side of the world, or your favorite tropical island and still stay connected to your clients, market, or customers.

Your employer may require you to be available during the usual work hours of a specific time zone and while that might translate into a 5am-1pm workday, but when you're off at 1pm, think of all that daylight time you have to explore the area you're traveling through! Or maybe your time zone will require you to work 2pm-10pm, which would allow you to sleep in and enjoy a leisurely breakfast before heading out to see what the world has to offer. Oftentimes when you work remotely you're granted the freedom to create your own schedule. There are a variety of programs, apps, habits, and practices that can smooth your transition into the telecommuting life.

Who should work remotely?

There's a certain breed of human who can pull this off successfully. Primarily, you must be self-motivated. If you're the guy/gal that slacks off when the boss is gone and you need direction in order to be productive this isn't for you. If you're the type who knows what has to get done and prefers to be left to it, you'll do nicely in a remote work environment.

In addition to discipline and time management you'll have to segregate social media for work and social media for personal use. This sounds like a no-brainer, but you'd be surprised how much time you respond to notifications while you're "working."

Finally, to work remotely, you must love what you do. This is the case with all work. If you hate your job day in and day out, now is the time to change your life. Whatever your skill set, you can find an alternative solution. You have to. If you stay in a job you loathe, you are wasting precious moments and can easily slide down the slippery slop to burnout (see our Prevention & Treatment of Burnout Course).

So what can you do?

Change your life.

Investigate if remote work is an option for you in your current job? If so, start now. Whatever has been holding you back, take a step forward toward achieving your goals. You might surprise yourself! Be the employee they don't want to lose and will do anything to keep.

Working remotely has benefits for both you and your employer. If your employer is hesitant to allow you to work remotely, employ the following plan:

Ask your boss for a 10 minute meeting at his earliest convenience. Prepare a powerpoint or video presentation where you address his/her concerns and prove why remote work is a win-win for you and your boss. Restrict your presentation to 5 key slides:

1. Employees who work from home take fewer personal and sick days

- Less stress = less sickness
- More time for exercise (due to the elimination of a commute)
- Decreased exposure to germs around the office (flu season won't take everyone out at once)

2. Remote workers are proven to be more productive than their office dwelling counterparts

3. Improved morale & employee retention

4. More money in the _____(company's) pocket:

- Decreased office space needs
- Saving in utilities
- Less hardware requirements, and IT upkeep
- Less phone lines and office equipment required for the same amount of work
- You can advertise your company as more environmentally friendly through the use of remote workers (less utilities and less people commuting to work)

5. In order to be considered for remote work an employee must: Create a list of requirements needed in order for an employee to work remotely. Treat it like a promotion, a reward for superior performance. For example:

- Have worked for at least 1 year with the company
- Have zero written or verbal warnings (empty file)
- Have access to a computer less than ___ years old, or with certain specs
- _____ Minimum internet speed required

- Apply for a remote work trial that can be approved or denied by management
- Demonstrate their ability for self-directed work with a one-month trial period where the employee works from home on Tuesdays and Thursdays

PLAN OF ACTION

Hopefully you've peaked his/her curiosity. At the end of the presentation hand your boss a Plan of Action that you've created to address further concerns and to show you mean business. You must demonstrate the initiative required to be an excellent remote worker from the get-go.

You can do this by creating a plan that includes: what technology you will be using at home (Type of computer, internet speed, programs/software, etc.), that you have a home office clear from distractions, share the current research proving the benefits and drawbacks of telecommuting, how you plan to avoid potential problems or communication breakdowns, and how you will safeguard proprietary information.

If at this point you are still shot down, I would capitalize on the trial period. Ask him what day of the week would be best to for a trial run. Make sure and deliver a high-visibility important project at the end of your day at home. Make it a show-stopper!

There are plenty of employers who would be oh-so-happy to add you to their location independent team. Businesses everywhere recognize the financial and productive benefits remote work offers, so if your boss doesn't fit the bill then upgrade to a more current model.

Lucky for you, working remotely isn't new. Below is the top 25 websites used to secure remote work:

THE TOP 25 REMOTE WORK WEBSITES

1. FlexJobs
FlexJobs has over 50 career categories, with jobs ranging from freelance to full-time, entry-level to executive. The best part? They screen the jobs before posting, so you don't have to dig through shady opportunities. The site currently hosts more than 20K job listings including part-time and freelance opportunities!

2. We Work Remotely
Sponsored by the creators of Remote: Office Not Required, this job board is a catch-all of remote jobs from customer service to web design to programming. This site is sure to host remote opportunities at some of the hottest tech companies.

3. Working Nomads
WorkingNomads (formerly goRemotely) delivers a curated list of remote jobs right to your inbox. Choose daily or weekly emails to make the remote job search come to you.

4. Staff.com
Instead of focusing on contract jobs, Staff.com features primarily long-term telecommuting jobs in a range of industries from personal assistants to programming. Choose to work either 80 hours a month (part-time) or 160 hours a month (full-time), and the site recruiters start matching you with employers!

5. Skip The Drive
With a great name, a great resources tab (listing authors to follow and sites to check for help in the remote job world), and a decent listing of remote jobs, this site is true to its eponymous mission. Use what the site provides, you can completely skip that ugly morning commute.

6. Virtual Vocations

This job board features only telecommuting jobs from technical writers to paralegals. Started by a stay-at-home mom frustrated with the job search for legitimate remote jobs, the company is still run by an entirely remote team. Plus, the blog has great tips, such as a recent article on how to take on a remote gig for the holiday season.

TECH

7. Authentic Jobs

The job board for web professionals. Just click the "wireless logo" (you'll recognize it) and filter by remote jobs. Beautifully designed and easy to use, as you'd expect from a job board for creatives and developers!

8. Dribble

Dribble is a great site for designers to find their next gig. There's a location tab right on top where you can click "remote / anywhere" and be off to the races finding your next work-from-home gig.

9. AngelList

Always dreamed of working for a startup, but don't live in a startup city hub? Head over to AngelList, a top site for startup jobs. When you search for a job on AngelList, click on "Job Type" and choose "Remote OK."

10. Stack Overflow

Stack Overflow is a go-to jobs board for many top tech talent, especially web developers. Type in "remote" in the location field and you'll bring up a list of more than 2,000 jobs that fit the bill.

11. Ruby Now
A job board entirely dedicated to Ruby developers. Once you graduate from the Web Developer Blueprint, and watch Adda's video on how to get hired as a Ruby Developer, head on over and get to work landing a remote gig here.

FREELANCE & CONTRACT

12. SkillBridge
Focused on connecting top-tier former consultants with short-term engagements for high impact corporations, the SkillBridge model is taking the traditional consulting world by storm. As a consultant, you can focus on only remote work and only on projects (and with clients) you are passionate about. Whether you bring e-mail marketing expertise or are a whiz at building financial models, the SkillBridge site and model is a remote-worker-dream-come-true.

13. Fiverr
With jobs starting at just $5 a pop, Fiverr is an amazing site to find your first gigs and build up a portfolio FAST. The site focuses on "gigs" or "micro-jobs," such as editing an image in photoshop, designing a Facebook ad, or brainstorming SEO-rank-worthy article titles.

14. Upwork
Upwork features remote jobs in a suite of categories: from virtual assistants to mobile app developers. A little something extra to sweeten the deal: Upwork claims that more than 1 million companies, from Pinterest to OpenTable, use the site to hire remote freelancers.

15. Guru

With the tagline "Work Your Way," Guru allows freelancers to build profiles with portfolios of work. Employers find your profile, or search/apply for jobs. The homepage features a wide range of roles from WordPress Developers to Logo Designers.

16. Elance

More than 300K programmers and more than 200K designers use Elance to connect with remote job opportunities. Upwork recently acquired Elance and oDesk! Microsoft, Cisco, and Mozilla are just a few of the companies hiring contract workers on Elance/ Upwork.

17. Freelancer.com

Claiming to be "The World's Largest Outsourcing Marketplace," Freelancer.com is chock full of remote freelancing gigs. With over 13 million users, it features jobs for PHP developers, content writers, and web designers alike. Make a profile and start bidding on jobs!

18. Freelancermap.com

Search thousands of IT projects that are remote, and almost always contract. This site has a global reach with projects at companies from Holland to Spain to Ohio!

GENERAL

19. The Muse

With a gorgeous user interface and fun-to-explore information about all the companies and jobs they feature, The Muse makes the job search easy. Search for the content features on the site that highlight remote opportunities, such as 7 Companies That Let You Work From Home.

20. Indeed
One of the most robust job boards you can find, Indeed pulls data from around the internet and around the world to bring together jobs. From Product Marketers to a "Technology Productivity Consultant," Indeed's 2K+ remote jobs run the gamut.

21. Idealist
For those who have always wanted to work on public health in Africa, or economic development in India, but weren't willing to uproot from your friends, family, and country, Idealist.org has the opportunities for you. You can filter all of your searches by selecting "remote" in the location category.

22. Career Builder
The Career Builder jobs site is the largest online employment website in the United States! Type in "telecommute" or "remote" as a keyword and find more than 9K part-time, contract, and full-time jobs from brands like Forever 21 Inc, Xerox, and Univision.

23. Monster
The first name you think of when you hear the words "job board," Monster does indeed host a plethora of remote jobs. From remote customer service opportunities to remote user experience designers, there are plenty of options if you're willing to sift.

DIRECT SELLING

24. Jewelry: Stella & Dot
This jewelry company has a "flexible entrepreneurship" model for stylists: host in-home or online trunk shows to display jewelry to friends. Flexibility and stye in one! If this doesn't fit your style, there are several jewelry companies providing this type of remote job opportunity including Chloe & Isabel andTrend Tribe.

25. PowerToFly

This new (but fast up-and-coming) site is a dream come true for tech woman around the world. PowerToFly is focused on matching women in tech with work-from-anywhere jobs. Join the talent database, go through the vetting process, and get matched for a "paid trial," a 2-4 week test period to make sure it's a good fit for both you and the employer. Started by two moms with serious tech chops, this company is perfectly poised to make your remote job dream a reality!

In order to work from the road, you'll need to establish a framework. This can include but is not limited to setting up an email account, online banking, international communication solutions, business numbers in each country code necessary, mail forwarding services, securing a US address, purchasing a laptop and any other devices required for connectivity to the internet.

After the basics are set up, you'll need to figure out when you're the most productive. On planes, trains, in coffee shops, or at home in a quiet space? You will have to be creative with time management so that your work play balance is healthy. Consider what you want your work hours to be. Are you more creative and productive in the morning or late at night? Do you want to treat your travel days like weekend days, or are you productive on the road? If you plan to incorporate travel in your regular life, you'll need to utilize offline time as best you can. While this world is incredibly accessible to the internet, there are times when you won't be connected while traveling, and where the internet is down. Applications like Google-Offline are helpful for managing your emails while not connected to the internet. Keep a list of the top 5 things you need to accomplish that don't require internet access.

Also, if you're not sure where you should work remotely from, Nomad List provides a great summary of the most important things for location independent workers.

WORKING SPACE

If the coffee shop doesn't float your boat there are more options. With the wave of telecommuters, wanderers, and freedom business owners comes a new wave in office space called co-working spaces. A collective office that rents an office, desk, or conference room by the day or hour!

There is a real variety of work spaces ranging from waterfront remote sites using solar power and satellite internet, to urban dwellers located with prime espresso service and climbing walls! Read this recent article describing 12 of the coolest work spaces around the world. There are a variety of sites dedicated to finding you the right workspace. Most of them focus on one city but there are a few below that are worldwide:

Desk Surfing
Impact Hub
Co-Working Visa
Regis
Share Desk

If in your recent past life you were an 8 to 5'er, it will take some time to adjust to the variety and freedoms allotted to those who work from the road. While it's a great change, it's change none the less. Even good stress wears at you. Be kind to yourself as you find your new groove. Keep making tweaks until you find what works best for you.

Most people feel their best with a regular sleep and rise schedule, a morning shower, eating breakfast, and getting dressed for the day before they attempt to contribute to society. This is still true if you work from home. Just because you can work in your PJs doesn't necessarily mean you should.

Don't neglect your self-care each day. Take time to exercise, eat, and take breaks. It's absolutely imperative that you have a start and stop time! Telecommuting doesn't mandate that you work 24 hours a day. Just because your office and laptop are one room away, doesn't mean you are on call 24/7. You need to set clear boundaries for yourself and those you work with. After all, you're roaming the world to go and explore, you don't want to get caught up working every single day! Creating a balanced schedule and sticking to it is key for a successful balance of life, family, and business.

A friend of mine, Corey Coates, owns a Podcast production company (Podfly) in addition to working for a second company as a program director. He shared,

"I start every workday early with yoga, meditation, and a light breakfast (fruit and yogurt). Then I work until lunch, when I leave for a stroll on the beach. I then return to work until 3:30pm, quitting time. I turn my phone off, close my laptop and don't think of work a minute after 3:30pm. That's the key to being as productive as I am, and not burned out."

Utilize Scheduling Tools

Explore these resources and see what works best for you.

RescueTime: This online resource tracks your productivity by measuring where you spend time on your computer. Once you download it, you can customize which websites and applications count as being productive, neutral, or unproductive. For example, I consider www.lifeanotherway.com to be a very productive website for me, while 9gag.com is considered to be very unproductive. If you track your computer activity with this app, you'll likely notice some interesting trends in your workday performance. You can discover what time of day you're most productive, which websites are distracting you, and how many hours you're actually on Facebook. When a graph is staring you in the face with startling high hours dedicated to social media, you might reconsider your work style and refocus your day. Unless you work in social media of course.

Asana: This online work tool allows for team members to communicate in one space for multiple projects and programs. Instead of keeping track of countless email threads, documents, and calendars. You can track everything and everyone in one location and everyone works in the same platform.

Any.Do: Is a decent task management tool you can keep on your smartphone to keep you focused. It can alert you and remind you to stay on track, especially given that most of us are pretty attached to those devices. Start your day with a list of tasks you've already created, the app sends a nice little Good Morning message to make those tasks seem more pleasant.

Hour Trackers: There are numerous apps that help you manually track your hours for various clients. Freelance/contract workers or those who do more face-time or phone-time with clients than email and computer work rely heavily on these. Hours Keeper is one commonly used tracker available on both iTunes and Android platforms. RescueTime tracks your computer usage. So if you're a website developer it will track your time spent building a website.

Reward Yourself

If you complete a task early, reward yourself. Whether it's with a fun break activity or a special night out on the town, do something that makes you smile. Reward systems are used in workplaces everywhere, so there's no need to cut it out just because you're not in a traditional office environment.

Find Balance

It's easy to lose sight of your schedule, and the line between work and home life can become blurred if you aren't careful. To avoid this, you must create a work/life balance that clearly delineates your focus time and your personal time. If you're required to work a certain number of hours in a day, make sure you log your focused work hours and don't let your work leak into your time off.

More often than not, the trouble isn't getting the remote worker to log enough hours due to lack of supervision, it's getting them to stop working. Remote workers often work many more hours than their office counterparts, partly due to the fact that their office is in their home. There is no clear line when work ends and their time off begins since they don't have to "leave work," unless they work hard to create one. That's why it's important to create these boundaries in order to prevent burnout.

IN THE END

You have to like what you're doing. I know someone who runs a waterfall business in Costa Rica. He leads tourist to some of the most beautiful waterfalls in the country and shows them how to cliff-dive into their pools. Almost every tour he's asked, "How did you get a job doing that?" when maybe they should have been asking "How do I create a job doing that?"

Additional Resources:

Books: Remote: Office Not Required,
Articles: Why Remote Teams Are the Future

COMMON TRAVEL-SIZED JOBS

I'll share with you some of the more common travel-sized careers, however, I don't want you to think you must enter one of these fields. You truly can travel-size most careers. Even physicians and surgeons are working from home with the help of robots!

WRITER

Freelance writing has long been a career that is ideal for the wanderer. Not only do you have the freedom to design your perfect day on the road but with all of your experiences you'll never run out of things to write about.

Make sure and initiate your writing business from your country of origin. You'll need to build a portfolio and be published several times in order to hone your skills and have a steady platform to leap from while on the road. Subscribe and or buy The Writer's Market. It's a directory published annually that includes the contact information, payment information, topics they publish, and query directions for each publisher. It's basically the writer's bible. Start locally and move your way up. Make sure you spend ample time learning how to write a query (taught in said book), and always follow submission guidelines.

If you're hoping to sell some of your images as well then also pick up the Photographer's Market, it guides you in the same way to sell your images.

CONSULTANT

If you have worked during your lifetime then you have experience in something. Think about what you're good at, and see if you can pull together a market you can help through consultations.

There are a variety of business opportunities abroad with new business owners in every sector. These new owners need help with a variety of niches: marketing, social media, customer service practices, IT, website development, content creators, multi-media, international accounting, productivity, import/export, etc

TEACHER

You can easily earn your TESOL or TEFL certificate online, in the classroom, in exotic locations around the world, or a combination of the two! This certificate makes you eligible for teaching jobs across the globe. Most employers require you to be a native English speaker and have taken a 120 hour course in either TESOL or TEFL. Some also require a Bachelor's degree in any subject.

While taking your TEFL certification, it's possible to specialize in "young learner" or "business English" thereby adding marketability and greater appeal to land a job in your preferred target audience.

Corey Coates, featured in our Becoming an Expat podcast, earned a TEFL certificate as his tool to enter an international life. He got a job teaching English in Costa Rica and quickly promoted through management positions until he landed as the director of education overseeing the operation of two countries! He later launched his own business but it all started with a TEFL certificate! I'm TEFL certified with a 120 unit course.

NON PROFITS / NGOs EMPLOYEE

The international NGO (non-government organization) community is enormous. Many of these organizations are in need of English speaking staff in administration, fundraising, marketing, and other job classifications. Monthly salaries can vary greatly. Telecommuting from these jobs isn't super popular yet, but you could try to consult for them or work as a temp.

WORK IN TOURISM

Tourism is a multi-billion dollar industry. As mentioned before, the baby boomers are just beginning to enter into their retirement as the wealthiest group the world has ever seen. What do they all have in common? They all want to travel.
Group travel has always sported a healthy market and is seeing large increases in demand. This means you could hop on an established tour group as a tour director after you earn your certificate through the International Guide Academy.

Or if you'd rather guide than direct, become a specialized guide for a niche group: LGBT, Food, Wine, Coffee, Grandparent, or Children tours to name a few. You can earn guide certification through the National Tour Association. In addition to an international license, you may need to obtain your certification as a tour guide from the Ministry of Tourism in your country.

If you're a behind the scenes kind of person and have an artistic eye, you can secure work designing those flashy tourism brochures and website content.

DESIGN / MARKETING

Creatives with an artistic gift are needed for businesses around the world. With Skype, screen sharing, and other technology it's really not necessary to meet in person.

The same goes for those skilled at building a marketing plan, campaign, product launch, or constructing general marketing content. Marketing is a huge market to tap into. There are hundreds of specialties you can zero in on. With time and a few campaigns under your belt you can become very marketable internationally.

A JOB AT EVERY STOP

Illegal or "under the table" jobs are offered across the globe in retail, restaurant, hospitality, and tourism sectors. This course does not endorse working illegally, it simply acknowledges that it occurs. Many wanderers gamble with work, banking on their chances at securing work at each location they spend longer stays in. They travel, drain their resources then set down for a few months, save up, and hit the road again. This is self-sustaining and works well for many (usually the younger work force) but is not for the faint of heart. Remember, this method requires you to job hunt under a high stress situation. Being broke is scary, being broke in a foreign country without the means to make it home is even more terrifying!

The people I have seen succeed with this method have been incredibly people oriented. The type that befriends a whole town in a matter of a week. That same skill is what earns them job offers at restaurants, hotels, and housesits.

WORK VISAS

Securing a work visa usually requires you to demonstrate that you are filling a position a local does not have the capabilities to fill (i.e. English language, healthcare, IT, Biotech, and International Business skills). Some countries require a bachelor's degree in the related field.

You will need a letter from the company hiring you specifying why they are contracting you and what importance you will bring to their company. Oftentimes, if you are being hired by an international company they will facilitate your entire immigration logistics.

LIVE FOR FREE

Whatever the reason, whatever your situation, it's possible so unless you're attached to the idea of paying rent, it would be crazy not to consider!

HOUSE-HOTEL-PET-SITTING

Exactly as it sounds, if you are a house, hotel, or pet sitter, you watch and maintain the property and animals per the instructions of the owner. If you do your homework right, this type of arrangement is a win win and can be an excellent way to save money while experiencing life as a local in a new area!

There is a huge range of responsibilities from one sitting job to another. Which is why it's imperative to ask all of the right questions, gather all the information, rules, and expectations before you commit to a job. Your tasks could range from watching a house and watering plants, to a rigorous pet activity and care program that requires something of you every couple of hours. Below are some examples of websites that advertise caretaking jobs. While options in EC exists, none of the sites exist solely for Ecuador and their inventory constantly turns over.

- MindmyHouse.com
$20/year

- HouseCarers.com

$50/year

This site has room for improvement, but is an excellent choice for those seeking a house in the land down under

- CareTaker.org

$30/year

I have personally used this site, and find that it has extensive listings. The downside is it doesn't allow you to view all of the listings without subscribing.

- TrustedHouseSitters.com

$49 for 3 months

$64.00 for 6 months

$79.00 for12 months

This site offers more listings than any of the others.

Word of Mouth & Part-Time Expats

Keep your eyes and ears open for opportunities to help other expats keep their home and pets safe while they visit family back home!

You will have to put forth some effort to land a house/pet sitting gig. After all, living for free is a pretty epic goal and competition can be fierce. The first job is often the hardest to land because you lack experience and pertinent references. The key to success is to look at each sitting opportunity as a job interview. Be professional, polite, and learn as much about the position as possible before you make any decisions.

The profile you create (with the service you subscribe to) is the equivalent of your resume. If you don't put in effort here, don't bother subscribing. Remember, these home and pet owners are looking for a stranger to welcome into their home when they aren't going to be there! Don't sound like a robot, be yourself in a respectable way and show passion. Let them get to know you through your profile.

Include examples that display how responsible you are: your hobbies, your cleanliness, pet enthusiasm, experience, your hobbies, and what you can do for them. Don't just say you like dogs, make sure and use examples demonstrating how much you care for animals (i.e. you're a volunteer for a local humane society). If you have horse, gardening, or farming experience, say so. If you haven't worked as a house/ pet sitter abroad, but have done so for family and friends include those experience and offer the references. If you have experience with www.couchsurfing.org, make sure to include that along with your user name then the homeowners can read your reviews as a guest and host on the site. When in doubt, ask for previous bosses, landlords, and even teachers to vouch for your trustworthiness and reliability.

Everyone has a special set of skills, if yours happens to be handy work, then mention it. Homeowners will feel better knowing their home will be cared for if something breaks while they are away. If you have gardening skills, marketing skills, computer skills, alternative energy skills, list them. You never know how your skills could benefit the homeowner. After all, the goal here is a mutually beneficial relationship!

Once you find a job you want to apply for, you have a chance to send a brief message along with your profile for their review. Treat this message like a cover letter. A brief introduction to what you can do for them, why their house is the job you want, and why they should hire you over other prospective sitters. Make sure to be passionate and real. Show your personality in a professional way.

Speaking of professionalism, make sure to respond quickly and professionally to each email correspondence. Write their name at the top, use full sentences, and always end your message with something to the effect of, "I appreciate your time and consideration."

Hesitation may cost you excellent housesitting opportunities. If the house is in a desirable location, the position will often be filled the same day it posts. Setting up alerts for your desired location could be the most important thing you do with your service.

Once you have captured a homeowner's interest and have answered their questions or concerns, don't neglect your own. You need to ask the right questions to insure the position is a good fit for you. Ask the owner:

- Is it ok to have guests?
- How long can the pet/house can be left alone? (You may wish to explore a nearby town for the weekend)
- Is there a vehicle you can use?
- What is public transit like near them?
- How far away is the nearest grocery store?
- Will you have access to the internet?
- Is there warm water?
- Are there any rules you need to abide by?

MASTERING SITTING

In order to be an excellent house/pet sitter, all that's required is common sense and fulfillment of the owner's requests. Remember, you're a guest so make sure you return the home in *better* condition than you received it. Wash the linens you used, make certain the house is tidy, and if you'd like some brownie points, make some brownies! Leave something homemade in the fridge for their arrival home with a note so they know you made it especially for them.

Pay close attention to the owner's requests. If the owner asks you to leave the mail in a certain area, take care to neatly place the mail in its designated place. If they'd like you to check in via email every so often, make sure and set an alarm in your calendar to do so. If you respect their wishes and go above and beyond the minimum expectation, you will accumulate an unending list of glowing references enabling a rent-free lifestyle for as long as you'd like.

WORK EXCHANGE

A work exchange is bartering work for accommodations. It's a great opportunity to see what it's like to live and work in a new region or with a new culture without taking financial risk.

Workaway.info and Helpx.net are two great websites that allow you to search for places to work in exchange for free room and board *(On the flip side, once you decide to buy a home, you can host workers through the site to help you remodel, or advertise a new business in exchange for room and board.)*

Just like housesitting, your profile matters! Take time to construct one that really draws on your skill-set. Next, search the country where you'd like to work and the type of work that you'd like to do.

For example, I searched Ecuador and organic farm stay. This resulted is a list of organic farm owners who were looking for some extra help in exchange for room and board. The range of work possibilities is extensive. Examples of work projects include: help with new construction, marketing, refurbishing a boat, gardening, cooking, teaching English, farming, housekeeping, concierge, working with horses, etc.

The most common arrangement I've seen advertised is approximately 20 hours of work in exchange for free room and board. I'd also say that farming both organic and in-organic offer the most jobs.

Make sure and clarify your specific arrangement with the owner because every situation is unique. Some work exchanges are full-time in exchange for free room and board and an additional stipend. I've seen others that want you to pay them for some of your expenses and work full time for them.

Free room and board is great, walking away from a few months living alongside a new culture, town, way of life, with a new skill, is priceless!

The Caretakers Gazette also offers work exchanges for a small stipend and free room and board. On that particular site, I've observed work as caregiver, handy-person, and live-in hotel manager most frequently.

COUCH SURFING

Couch surfing is not just a way to describe sleeping on your cousin's couch any longer. Now, it is an entire genre of travel. People of all ages travel around the world meeting Couch Surfers from every country they've traveled.

Couch surfing is a free short-term local housing solution. The average stay is two nights. It's a great way to travel around EC searching for the region that best suits you, and gathering information and advice from locals and expats who have already made the move.

www.CouchSurfing.org is a site whose slogan is, *"Changing the world one couch at a time."* To experience this new way of travel, all you need to do is sign up and create a free profile. There, you can decide whether you'd like to host travelers, play tour guide, or simply chat over a cup of joe, and exchange stories.

You're never required to host someone, even if your profile says that you can. You can search for potential hosts, or for *surfers* looking for a place to stay in your area. If you find a "couch" you'd like to surf, simply write to them.

In your couch surfing request, tell them why you'd like to stay with them in particular. Show them that you took the time to read their profile.

Even though it's called "couch" surfing, oftentimes your host has a spare bedroom you can have all to yourself! The sleeping situation is listed in the profile of the potential host. I've couch surfed in Canada, St. Lucia, and across the United States. I have hosted surfers many times in Costa Rica and had excellent experiences making friends with travel peers around the world!

ADDITIONAL READING
- *Work Your Way Around the World: The Globetrotter's Bible* by Susan Griffith
- *The Work From Home Handbook* by Diana Fitzpatrick and Stephen Fishman

HEALTHCARE

Healthcare is a big deal for most. Take a look at elections across the globe, a leading promise is always to better healthcare. Why? Because it matters. We want the assurance if we get sick and are in need of care or a life saving procedure, we will have access. In addition to a language and culture barrier, Ecuador has a health system unfamiliar to expats. So let's get familiar with it, shall we?

Healthcare is quirky and personal. Each individual's comfort level will vary. Some folks prefer to pay out of pocket and others choose to purchase a combination of public, private, and international healthcare insurances. Each plan carries a corresponding price tag and peace of mind.

PREVENTION

Below are a few friendly, illness prevention techniques:

- Take daily walks through your new natural oasis and see your mood, energy level, bone density, Vitamin D levels, and health improve.
- Replace sugar drinks and beer with fresh coconut water (coco helado) and smoothies made from the ridiculously delicious produce.

VACCINATIONS

It's a good idea to go to a travel clinic or schedule an appointment with your doctor in order to discuss and receive vaccinations for the countries you anticipate visiting. The CDC recommends[1] the following vaccinations:

- Hepatitis A
- Typhoid
- Hepatitis B
- Rabies *(for those who plan to work with dogs, live in remote areas, adventure travel, or caving)*
- Yellow Fever required if entering Ecuador from Peru or Colombia *(Recommended for the following provinces east of the Andes Mountains less than 2300 m in elevation: Morona-Santiago, Napo, Orellana, Pastaza, Sucumbios, and Zamora-Chinchipe. Also reccommend for travel to the following provinces west of the Andes and less than 2300 m in elevation - Esmeraldas, Guayas, Los Rios, Manabi, and designated areas of Azuay, Bolivar, Canar, Carchi, Chimborazo, Cotopaxi, El Oro, Imbabura, Loja, Pichincha, and Tungurahua - recommended only for those at risk for a large number of mosquito bites. Not recommended for travel limited to areas greater than 2300 m in elevation, the cities of Guayaquil and Quito, or the Galápagos Islands. Required for travelers arriving from a yellow-fever-infected area in Africa or the Americas).* Just get it.

---

[1] http://wwwnc.cdc.gov/travel/destinations/traveler/none/ecuador

If you have any questions or other concerns about vaccinations and other health precautions (i.e. safe food, water practices, and insect bite protection) call the Centers for Disease Control and Prevention's hotline: 1-877-FYI-TRIP (1-877-394-8747).

CARE

Sometimes, the right healthcare option for you is a matter of comfort. If you've had the same cardiologist or family practitioner for years, you have a history and trust that was built over the course of many years. Moving abroad will complicate things. Be prepared to have an open mind. If continuity is important then you will need to select a doctor or two near your travel bases in order to have them oversee your care. I highly recommend you interview doctors in your potential home base regions. Make an appointment and interview specialists that are applicable to your needs.

INTERVIEW YOUR DOCTOR:

☐Where did they complete schooling?
☐Are they board certified? *(All physicians are licensed but not all are board certified.)* If so, in what specialty?
☐How many patients have they had with my particular ailment/condition?
☐How can you reach them outside of office hours? Cell phone number?
☐Do they respond to calls during office hours?
☐If they are out of town, who fills in for them?

ECUADOR EXPERIENCE

"The U.S. medical services are driven by the insurance companies. There, I was seen by my family provider, who referred me to an ENT. The ENT said I was grinding my teeth at night – referred me to a dentist (I do twice a year visits to my dentist). He immediately knew that was not the case and referred me to another ENT who stated that I needed to wear a mouth guard at night. Back to my family doctor, I get referred to get an MRI. MRI shows nothing. Back to the family doctor and 10 years of the back and forth with no results.

My experience here in Ecuador was positive; the care was spectacular. House calls are the norm at no additional cost. I got a sonogram, CAT scan (revealing a benign tumor), biopsy, pain medicine, and results (yes, that is a big deal). The cost of the whole lot was about $500. Dr. Elke speaks English; Dr. Victor is her husband. I called Dr. Elke and she did my initial visit. We then worked with Dr. Victor and Dr. Elke translated.

We used the dental services here and were pleased. It's quite simple – call and make an appointment. But, when you get to your appointment, be prepared to be seen. Not like in the states where you wait for hours. Nope, you are at 10:00, you are in the chair at 10:00."

~ Diane & Mark Bublack, expats from Houston

☐What is their philosophy of healthcare?
☐Do they have more than one location to see patients?
☐How do they handle billing?

After you have collected all of your information with at least three physicians (preferably those you have been referred to), decide what questions and answers hold the most stout with you and score them accordingly. Don't forget to weigh in heavily with your comfort level and rapport with your future physician.

OUT OF POCKET

Healthcare is cheap in some countries that many healthy folks opt to pay out of pocket! This is a common path for younger and healthy expats. Be warned, however, I know of an expat who fell and broke his hip. All said and done, he paid over $20,000 (including surgery, treatment of anemia, physical therapy, and months of rehab).

If you are concerned about cost, feel free to call the hospital where you would go and ask them the costs of a variety of procedures. They have a fee schedule and will tell you the cost.

INTERNATIONAL HEALTHCARE

If you don't plan to live in any one place full time or you travel so much you're barely at home, an international plan might be a better option for you.

Make sure the coverage that you choose has coverage inside the US if you think you may need to return within the given time period. Many insurances omit the US due to the inflated healthcare expenses.

BROKERFISH
www.brokerfish.com

This is a search option that you can use just like searching for airfare or car insurance. You enter in the ages of your family members and your desired international coverage. The most expensive factors seem to be whether or not you wish to have coverage in the US and whether or not you want to include emergency evacuation.

TRAVEL INSURANCE

If you don't plan to "stay put" for longer than 6 months at any given time then travel insurance may be your best option. An added bonus to purchasing travel insurance is besides coverage for your own flesh and bones, you can opt for insurance against lost luggage, trip cancellation, and sometimes theft! It also might be an ideal option for the roamer.

MEDEX

www.medexassist.com

I asked for a quote for two US citizen travelers ages 64 and 50 set to travel to Ecuador for exactly 5 months. The cost for each of them was $517 for five months coverage, totaling $1,034 for their stay in Ecuador. What do you get for your money?

- Up to $250,000 coverage
- $100 deductible per incident
- Includes medical evacuation and repatriation
- Includes accidental death and dismemberment
- Coverage for controlled pre-existing conditions
- 71 and under
- No hazardous sports coverage
- Trip cancellation coverage
- To see a full outline of coverage see: http://bit.ly/medexti

MEDICAL TOURISM

Three per cent of the *world*'s population travels internationally for medical treatment![2] That's roughly 211,710,000 people! Patients Beyond Borders, an organization that publishes international medical travel guidebooks, reported that the medical tourism industry produces $40 billion a year in business.

---

[2] IPK International Survey

Patients requiring elective, non-elective, and dental procedures are heading to Ecuador. Procedures are often less than half the cost in the United States.

The medical tourism industry capitalizes where the US lacks, offering numerous cosmetic and medical procedures for a fraction of the cost in the U.S. Some will also make your travel arrangements and their VIP services will take you by hand to everywhere you need to be.

BOOKS
Patients Without Borders: Everybody's Guide to Affordable, World-Class Healthcare[3]

---

[3] http://bit.ly/guidetohealthcare

THE MOVING BLUES

"Accept that in the first few months you may be brought to tears by the most innocuous of things. This doesn't mean you are going mad or failing; it's just part of the journey of adjustment to massive change. Cry when you need to then be determined to make the best of the next day."
~ Johanna: Irish Nomad in Malaysia

Some international residents have grown bitter and disgruntled. The most common cause is hyper-fixation on differences and change. They're like salmon, they flow along with all of the excitement and arrive to a fertile paradise abroad and the party is on! Shortly thereafter, they realize it is not what they thought it would be and flip a 180. They swim upstream fighting the way things are, and fighting the nature of the country they are in that once attracted them. They're left exhausted and eventually caught, and served for dinner.

In order to have a healthy relationship, you must love your partner for exactly the person they are today with their faults, their gifts, and everything in-between. So too, you must appreciate each country you reside in for exactly what it is today in order to live a healthy and happy life here.

I'm hopping off of my soap box now...

In every move I've made, I experienced a roller coaster of emotions. If you plan for it, it can take the edge off *a little*. Expect to have an initial high followed by an intense low. The low is mostly due to loneliness, culture shock which will be discussed next, and inaccurate expectations.

Change causes stress no matter what kind of stress it is. Moving to an amazing country that fits you perfectly is still a stressful event. There are concerns you will have and worries of endless logistics: luggage, pets, new house, new area, language acquisition, new foods, access to utilities, etc.

A key method for quick acclimation is to go out and make friends in the community. Find out the inner workings of the community and how you can contribute! If you spend all day interacting with those you left back home on Skype or magicJack then you've only left in body and are cheating your experience.

CULTURE SHOCK

This is not a phenomena that happens to the weak. It can slug you in the face or slowly tighten around you like a boa constrictor! Merriam - Webster describes culture shock as, "A sense of confusion and uncertainty sometimes with feelings of anxiety that may affect people exposed to an alien culture or environment without adequate preparation."

There are four stages of culture shock, much like grief.

- Honeymoon phase

- Negotiation phase

- Adjustment phase

- Mastery phase

Honeymoon Phase

The honeymoon phase is the high I mentioned earlier. No wrong could be done to you or by you. You're romanticized by the differences in the culture, pace, way of life, and new exotic foods. Just like the honeymoon phase in a new relationship, you are blinded to any faults of your lover's. Not until the dust settles does their obnoxious habits start to crawl under your skin, and you see the real them.

When your electricity goes out in a storm, or your water gets shut off for a day or two, or you are overcharged for a service and you can't get anyone to help fix it, those not-so-sexy parts of international bureaucracy sneak up and bite you.

Negotiation Phase

This is when reality settles in. When you sit down and wonder what have you done? All of the differences initially seen as romantic are all of the sudden cause for great concern. Can you really do this? Can you adjust to so many differences?

You realize how incredibly far away you are from "home" and your family. Maybe you don't know a soul abroad. If you aren't fluent in the local language, that carries with it an invisible wall. While you can't see the wall, you feel it in every interaction. You feel it when you have trouble ordering meat at the butcher counter, or paying your water bill, finding the sugar in the supermarket, or asking the bus driver how much is the fare. Additionally, it can be hard to adjust to new climates and new cuisine.

This phase is not pleasant and those who successfully navigate through it are gentle and patient with themselves. They also laugh at their mistakes, learn from others, and resolve that they are no longer in a hurry and no longer in the US. They learn and adopt realistic expectations.

Adjustment Phase

During this phase you have become accustomed to some of the new changes, like how long it takes to get your food while eating out and the long lines at the bank. You no longer fight the changes, you become accepting and build your routine around them. The changes become your new normal. Your understanding of the culture becomes more in-depth here, and you begin to cultivate connections with the community.

Mastery Phase

You feel 100% comfortable in your new culture. You accept the practices and participate in many aspects of the culture. You may not completely lose your culture of origin, but you are now an expert in the Ecuadorian way. You can navigate through any hurdle or problem as they arise knowing the appropriate course of action. You are ready to take a new expat under your wing and pass forward the experiences and knowledge that countless expats gave to you.

TIP
Remember, being an adventurer is not a race or a competition. It doesn't matter if you've lived abroad for 16 years and your new friend has only been abroad for one. It seems like many nomads want to pull out a measuring stick so they can find their place in the pecking order. Focus instead on what you have in common and enjoy each other's company.

If you're looking to move abroad check out our expat guidebook series: Becoming an Expat

Becoming an Expat: Costa Rica

Becoming an Expat: Thailand

Becoming an Expat: Mexico

Becoming an Expat Ecuador

Becoming an Expat 101

Becoming a Nomad